# SLAMMED BY
# TSUNAMIS

CAITIE MCANENEY

**PowerKiDS**
press
New York

Published in 2018 by The Rosen Publishing Group, Inc.
29 East 21st Street, New York, NY 10010

First Edition

Editor: Melissa Ráe Shofner
Book Design: Reann Nye

Photo Credits: Cover, pp. 1, 19 The Asahi Shimbun/Getty Images; pp. 4–30 (background) (c) Jon Sheer. All Rights Reserved./Moment/Getty Images; p. 4 bjul/Shutterstock.com; p. 5 Tony Craddock/Shutterstock.com; p. 7 GREGORY BOISSY/AFP/Getty Images; p. 8 Vince Streano/Corbis Documentary/Getty Images; p. 9 Peter Hermes Furian/Shutterstock.com; p. 11 Pasha_Barabanov/Shutterstock.com; p. 13 Philip Stephen/Nature Picture Library/Getty Images; p. 14 AFP/Getty Images; pp. 15, 27 YASUYOSHI CHIBA/AFP/Getty Images; p. 17 KAZUHIRO NOGI/AFP/Getty Images; p. 18 Chris McGrath/Getty Images News/Getty Images; p. 20 S009/Gamma-Rapho/Getty Images; p. 21 Paula Bronstein/Getty Images News/Getty Images; p. 23 Bloomberg/Getty Images; p. 25 ultrapok/Shutterstock.com; p. 26 XINHUA/Gamma-Rapho/Getty Images; p. 29 CHOO YOUN-KONG/AFP/Getty Images.

Cataloging-in-Publication Data

Names: McAneney, Caitie.
Title: Slammed by tsunamis / Caitie McAneney.
Description: New York : PowerKids Press, 2018. | Series: Natural disasters: how people survive | Includes index.
Identifiers: ISBN 9781538326541 (pbk.) | ISBN 9781538325650 (library bound) | ISBN 9781538326558 (6 pack)
Subjects: LCSH: Tsunamis-Juvenile literature. | Natural disasters-Juvenile literature.
Classification: LCC GC221.5 M44 2018 | DDC 551.46'37-dc23

Manufactured in the United States of America

CPSIA Compliance Information: Batch #BW18PK: For Further Information contact Rosen Publishing, New York, New York at 1-800-237-9932

# CONTENTS

# WHAT IS A TSUNAMI?

Imagine you're standing on a beautiful beach. Suddenly, the ocean seems to be sucked back. You can see fish flopping on the open ocean floor. Then, a giant wave builds and approaches the beach. Watch out—it's a tsunami!

A tsunami is a series of huge ocean waves. Each wave can reach 100 feet (30.5 m) tall or more. These waves can travel thousands of miles very quickly. Sometimes they reach speeds of 500 miles (804.7 km)

## DISASTER ALERT!

Some **geologists** believe an asteroid landing in the Indian Ocean caused a megatsunami, or huge tsunami, that hit Madagascar 10,000 years ago. Waves could have been as high as 300 feet (91.4 km).

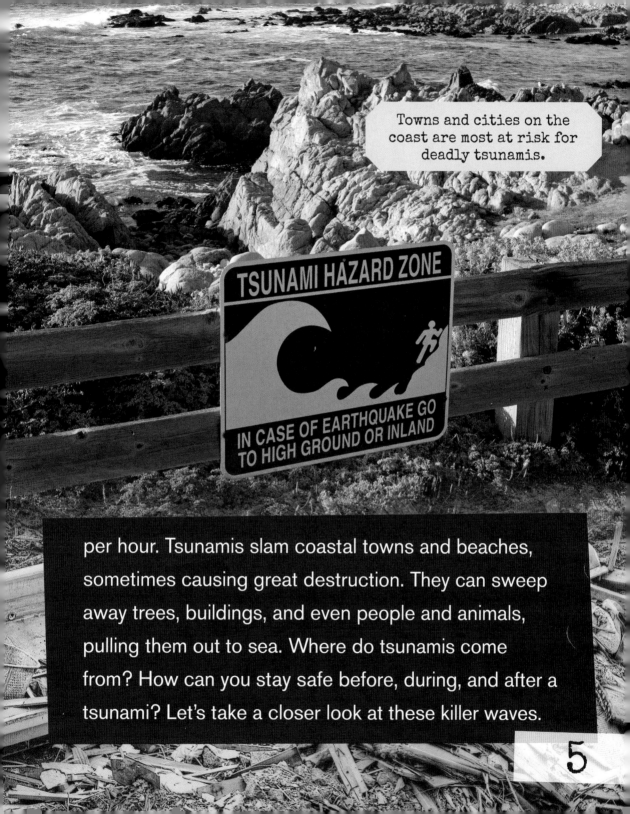

Towns and cities on the coast are most at risk for deadly tsunamis.

TSUNAMI HAZARD ZONE

IN CASE OF EARTHQUAKE GO TO HIGH GROUND OR INLAND

per hour. Tsunamis slam coastal towns and beaches, sometimes causing great destruction. They can sweep away trees, buildings, and even people and animals, pulling them out to sea. Where do tsunamis come from? How can you stay safe before, during, and after a tsunami? Let's take a closer look at these killer waves.

# TSUNAMI TRIGGERS

You've probably seen normal-sized waves at the beach. They rise up and crash along the shore, dragging pebbles and shells into the ocean. These waves are usually caused by wind over the ocean. In most cases, they only travel at about 56 miles (90 km) per hour. These waves usually don't cause damage.

Tsunamis happen when there's a **disturbance** that causes water to be quickly displaced, or moved. Tsunamis may be caused by underwater landslides, volcanic eruptions, or, most often, earthquakes. An earthquake in the middle of the ocean may drop or lift the ocean floor. This movement makes the water rise and form a wave. The wave may build and start to travel across the ocean toward the nearest coastline.

## DISASTER ALERT!

The word "tsunami" means "great harbor wave" in Japanese. Japan is one of the places in the world that's most affected by tsunamis.

Normal ocean waves don't pose too much of a risk to people. Some people even surf on them!

# IT'S TECTONIC!

Earthquakes cause tsunamis, but what causes earthquakes? Thousands of earthquakes happen every day. There are several million earthquakes each year. We usually don't feel small ones, but large earthquakes can cause a great amount of destruction.

Earth's outer shell—the lithosphere—is split into pieces called tectonic plates. The plates float on a layer

## DISASTER ALERT!

People who study earthquakes are called seismologists. Seismologists have special equipment to record earthquakes.

There are about 15 major tectonic plates on Earth. There are also many smaller plates.

JUAN DE FUCA PLATE

NORTH AMERICAN PLATE

EURASIAN PLATE

PACIFIC PLATE

PACIFIC PLATE

COCOS PLATE

CARIBBEAN PLATE

ARABIAN PLATE

INDIAN PLATE

PHILIPPINE PLATE

AFRICAN PLATE

NAZCA PLATE

SOUTH AMERICAN PLATE

AUSTRALIAN PLATE

ANTARCTIC PLATE

SCOTIA PLATE

of hot, soft rock, and they're always moving. Plates may move together or apart. Sometimes they slip past each other, grinding their way into a new position. This grinding, coming together, or moving apart causes pressure to build up. When this pressure is released suddenly, an earthquake occurs. When a big earthquake happens underwater, plates may move over or under each other. This sudden movement can displace a lot of water and cause a tsunami.

# THE RING OF FIRE

The more plate movement in a certain place, the greater the number of earthquakes that occur there. This is especially true in the Ring of Fire in the Pacific Ocean. This area features a string of volcanoes that developed due to tectonic plate movement. In fact, 75 percent of all active volcanoes on Earth are found here, and nearly 90 percent of all earthquakes happen here. Therefore, this is the area most affected by tsunamis.

The Ring of Fire is shaped like an upside-down "U." It stretches from the southern tip of South America up the West Coast of North America to the Bering Strait and down past Japan and New Zealand. People living near the Ring of Fire are always on alert for earthquakes, volcanic eruptions, and tsunamis.

**DISASTER ALERT!**
More than 452 volcanoes make up the Ring of Fire.

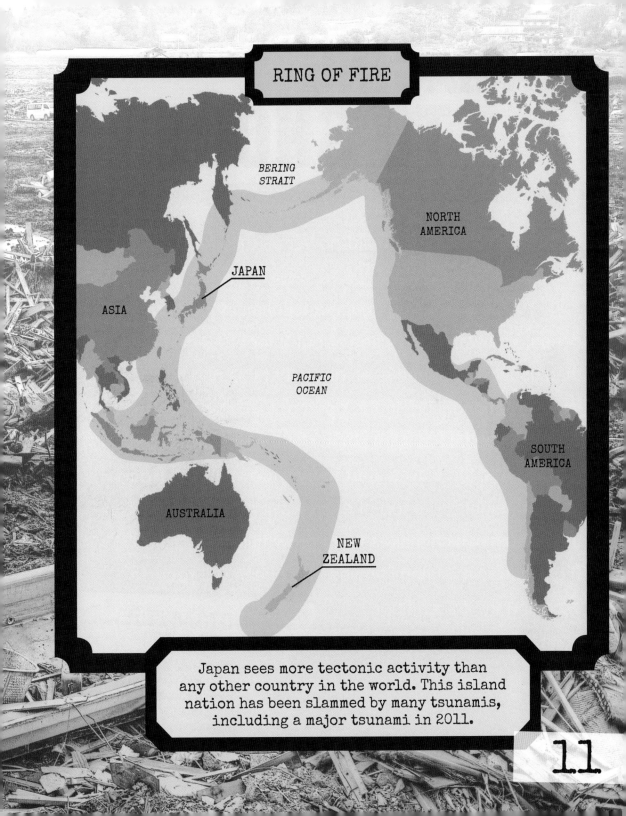

# RING OF FIRE

BERING STRAIT

NORTH AMERICA

JAPAN

ASIA

PACIFIC OCEAN

AUSTRALIA

NEW ZEALAND

SOUTH AMERICA

Japan sees more tectonic activity than any other country in the world. This island nation has been slammed by many tsunamis, including a major tsunami in 2011.

# RACING TO SHORE

An earthquake is only the birth of a tsunami. From there, the waves build power as they race toward the coasts.

You may not even notice a tsunami in the open ocean. The water only rises about 3 feet (0.9 m) higher than usual. The ocean is so deep that this rise may largely go unnoticed. In the open ocean, these waves can travel as fast as a jet plane. As the ocean's depth **decreases**, the waves start to slow down and build to greater heights. The top of each wave moves faster than the bottom, which makes them grow taller very quickly. Right before a tsunami arrives, the ocean will **recede**, exposing the ocean floor.

Then, the first wave hits.

## DISASTER ALERT!

It may be tempting, but never walk out onto the exposed ocean floor when the water recedes before a tsunami. This can be very dangerous since it means a tsunami is on the way.

Rogue waves have been part of seafaring stories for hundreds of years.

## Rogue Waves

Rogue waves are also called freak waves or killer waves. They're different from tsunamis because they form when swelling waves join together. Rogue waves seem to come out of nowhere. They're more than twice the size of the waves around them. People who see rogue waves are usually on ships far out in the ocean. Witnesses have said these waves look like a wall of water. It's hard to measure or study rogue waves because they're rare and unexpected.

# TSUNAMI DESTRUCTION

Once a tsunami slams onto shore, it can cause a great amount of destruction. Ships and fishing boats close to shore may be pushed miles inland. People and animals on shore are swept up and thrown down and may also be pulled into the ocean. Homes and other buildings along the coastline are **pummeled** and sometimes destroyed. Telephone lines, power lines, and bridges may

## DISASTER ALERT!

Smaller tsunami waves may only seem like a fast-moving tide. Tsunamis aren't tidal waves, though. They actually don't have anything to do with tides.

14

One reason tsunamis are so dangerous is because they move a lot faster than a person can run.

collapse. Cars and trees may be picked up and carried away by the water.

Massive flooding may reach miles away from shore. In a powerful tsunami, the first wave alone may destroy everything in its path. A tsunami is not just one wave, but a series of waves. The waves may continue to slam the shore for hours.

15

After the tsunami waves end, its destruction remains. The entire **infrastructure** of a town or city may be ruined, leaving people homeless and without supplies such as food and clean drinking water. Tsunamis that hit small islands may leave the landscape unrecognizable.

Tsunamis cause massive flooding, which can interfere with sewage and drinking water systems. Floodwater that's full of sewage can spread disease. Diseases such as malaria are spread by mosquitoes, which live near standing water. People may die because of a lack of clean water to drink and use.

Tsunamis are deadly for animals, too. Animals may drown, and the plants and trees of their **habitat** may be ruined. Pollution and waste from the shore may be pulled out into the sea, which can harm marine animals.

16

## DISASTER ALERT!

Toxic materials may be left behind after a tsunami. People have to be careful not to touch **debris** that could be harmful or deadly.

After a tsunami, a person's home might be gone and their community may not be safe to return to.

# TSUNAMI IN JAPAN, 2011

Japan has seen many tsunamis, but one of the most damaging tsunamis hit on March 11, 2011. A powerful earthquake off Japan's main island sparked a killer tsunami. It was one of the strongest earthquakes ever recorded.

A 33-foot (10 m) wave slammed into the coastal city of Sendai. One wave rushed about 6 miles (9.7 km) inland. Other cities, coastal towns, and regions were also

## DISASTER ALERT!

Japan's early warning system gave people about a one-minute notice before the earthquake occured. This doesn't sound like much time, but it saved many lives.

The Fukushima nuclear disaster showed how man-made waste and products could make tsunami destruction more serious than ever before.

hit. One of these regions was Fukushima, the site of a nuclear power plant. The tsunami caused explosions at the plant and a harmful release of nuclear **radiation**. **Contaminated** water leaked into the ocean, and people living around the nuclear power plant had to leave their homes. Nearly 16,000 people died in the 2011 Japan tsunami, and more than 2,500 people are still missing.

# INDIAN OCEAN TSUNAMI, 2004

On December 26, 2004, the world saw the worst tsunami in recorded history. Most tsunamis occur in the Pacific Ocean, but this unexpected disaster came from far out in the Indian Ocean. A powerful earthquake occurred near the island of Sumatra, which is part of Indonesia. Massive waves moved out in all directions.

Several countries were hit, including Thailand. Many tourists there had never seen the ocean recede so much.

**DISASTER ALERT!**

The 2004 tsunami reached Africa—nearly 3,000 miles (4,828 km) away.

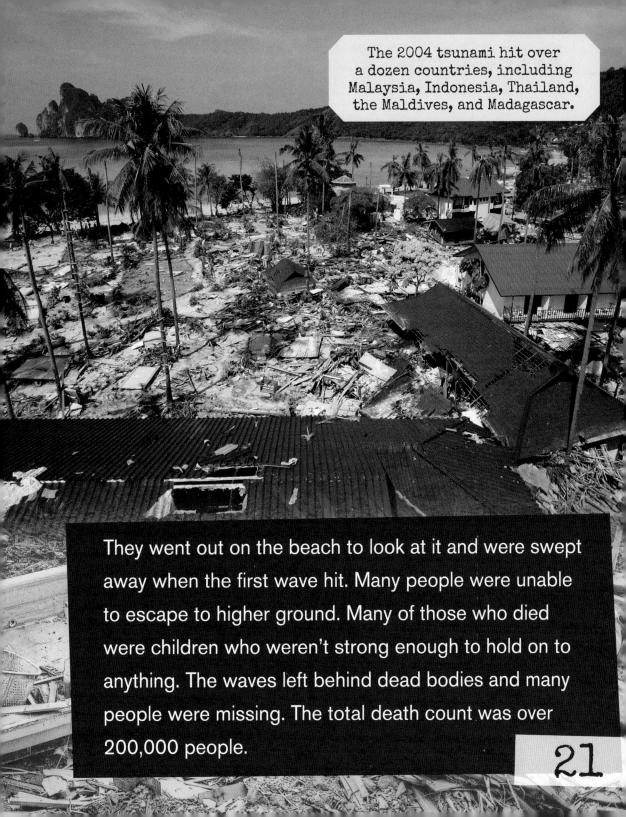

The 2004 tsunami hit over a dozen countries, including Malaysia, Indonesia, Thailand, the Maldives, and Madagascar.

They went out on the beach to look at it and were swept away when the first wave hit. Many people were unable to escape to higher ground. Many of those who died were children who weren't strong enough to hold on to anything. The waves left behind dead bodies and many people were missing. The total death count was over 200,000 people.

21

# PREDICTING
# A TSUNAMI

**Predicting** tsunamis is more important than ever. With more people living in bigger cities and towns along coasts, predicting when a tsunami will hit can save many lives.

The Pacific Tsunami Warning Center (PTWC) in Hawaii is one of the greatest tsunami watch groups in the world. Experts there study seismic, or earthquake, activity. They also look at data about the ocean's conditions. If it seems that a tsunami is possible, the PTWC warns all areas that may be in danger. Some at-risk places alert people through text messages and other warning systems. Tsunami sirens, or alarms, may go off to warn people to get to a safe place. After the 2004 tsunami, the PTWC started to look out for danger in the Indian Ocean.

## DISASTER ALERT!

The United States established the PTWC in 1949 as part of its first efforts to create an official tsunami warning system.

Tsunami warnings can save thousands of lives. This is a tsunami siren tower in Indonesia.

## Animals Sense Tsunamis

Can animals sense tsunamis? Reports from the 2004 tsunami indicate that animals knew something was about to happen. Elephants reportedly ran for higher ground. Dogs and zoo animals refused to leave their homes or shelters. Some animals, including elephants, are tuned into vibrations in the ground, which could give them a clue when something is wrong. Other animals have strong senses of smell and hearing that may allow them to sense a disaster before it happens.

23

# GET TO HIGHER GROUND!

If you get a tsunami warning in an at-risk area, it's time to get to higher ground. Beaches and low-lying areas aren't safe. Since tsunamis can rush miles inland, people who can't even see the ocean should still listen to the warning. You could run up a large hill, away from the beach. You will probably only have a few minutes to do this, so it's good to have a plan ahead of time.

Some people become stuck inside buildings. However, if a tall building is made of sturdy material, such as concrete, you can go to the highest point to find safety. Most small buildings, such as houses, aren't safe and may be destroyed. Many places have **evacuation sites** for people to go to in case of emergency.

## DISASTER ALERT!

People in boats out at sea should stay in deep water if a tsunami hits land. People in small boats near a port should leave their boats and move to higher ground.

This **tsunami** evacuation building in Thailand gives people a safe place to run to in the event of a tsunami.

## Tsunami Education Saves Lives

Tourists in Thailand on December 26, 2004, weren't expecting a tsunami to hit. Many came from parts of the world that aren't at risk for tsunamis. Tilly Smith, a 10-year-old British girl, saw the water receding on the beach. While others looked interested, the girl knew that something was wrong. She thought of a lesson she learned in school about tsunamis. The girl yelled for everyone to leave the beach, saving her family and others.

# SAVING PEOPLE FROM TSUNAMIS

Tsunamis can cause total destruction. How can people help after a tsunami? Search-and-rescue teams go to the site of a tsunami as soon as the waves stop completely. They search through the wreckage for survivors. People and animals may be trapped under debris or in damaged buildings. Others may be floating in the open ocean, waiting to be rescued. Some people may be seriously hurt and need to be rushed to a hospital or

## DISASTER ALERT!

The International Rescue Committee is one of the organizations that helped survivors of the 2011 tsunami that hit Japan.

have their wounds treated at the site. Aid organizations send fresh food, water, and other supplies to areas that have been hit by tsunamis.

Help for tsunami victims doesn't stop after the debris is cleared away. Buildings, homes, and industries need to be rebuilt, which can take years. Transportation, communication, and utility systems, such as water and electricity, may also need to be restored.

# A FORCE OF NATURE

The National Oceanic and Atmospheric Administration (NOAA) reports that tsunamis have killed more than 420,000 people since 1850. In 2004 alone, tsunamis in the Indian Ocean left 1.7 million people homeless. Many remained homeless for years after. Many people were reported missing, possibly swept out into the ocean. Tsunamis can leave behind disease, **poverty**, and a great sense of loss. They're a danger to people in coastal towns and cities, especially in the Ring of Fire.

Tsunamis are proof that natural disasters can cause some of the greatest destruction on Earth. As with hurricanes and earthquakes, there's nothing humans can do to stop tsunamis from happening. The only thing we can do is be prepared. These giant waves are truly a deadly force of nature.

## DISASTER ALERT!

Other natural disasters, such as hurricanes and blizzards, may be predicted days ahead of time. Tsunamis may only be predicted a few minutes ahead of time.

The flooding from a tsunami may stick around for weeks. This picture shows a village slammed by the 2004 Indian Ocean tsunami, two weeks after it happened.

# TSUNAMI SAFETY TIPS

## The danger isn't over after an tsunami. Follow these tips to stay safe:

- If you're in an area at risk for tsunamis, plan a path from your location to higher ground. If you get a warning, move to higher ground as quickly as possible.

- After a tsunami, don't return to a coastal area until you've been told it's safe.

- If you hear a tsunami is coming, don't stay to watch it. If you can see the wave, you won't be able to escape it.

- If you see ocean water receding, get to higher ground.

- If an earthquake occurs offshore, find an evacuation route just in case.

- If you're in a tall building and can't leave for higher ground, go to the highest floor possible.

- After a tsunami, stay away from damaged buildings, debris, and fallen power lines.

# GLOSSARY

**contaminated:** Polluted.

**debris:** Broken pieces of objects.

**decrease:** To get smaller or become less.

**disturbance:** An upset to the natural position or arrangement of something.

**evacuation site:** A place where people go for safety during a disaster.

**geologist:** Someone who studies the history of Earth as shown through its rocks, soil, and landforms.

**habitat:** The natural home for plants, animals, and other living things.

**infrastructure:** The system of public works for a country, state, or region.

**poverty:** The state of being poor.

**predict:** To guess what will happen in the future based on facts or knowledge.

**pummel:** To pound or beat.

**radiation:** Waves of energy. Nuclear radiation is harmful to humans.

**recede:** To move back or away.

# INDEX

# WEBSITES

Due to the changing nature of Internet links, PowerKids Press has developed an online list of websites related to the subject of this book. This site is updated regularly. Please use this link to access the list: www.powerkidslinks.com/natd/tsun